Contents

Some words are shown in bold, **like this**.
You can find out what they mean by looking in the glossary.

Introduction

Most of Egypt is a desert of sand and rocks. The River Nile runs through it from south to north. People who came to Egypt usually lived beside the river, because it was the only place where crops could grow.

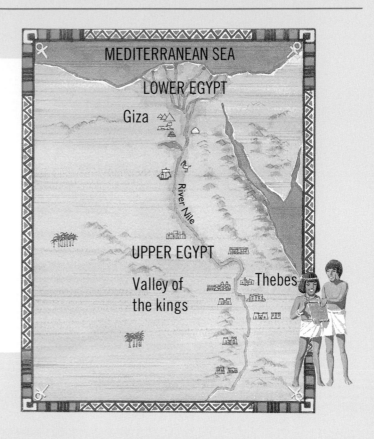

MEDITERRANEAN SEA

LOWER EGYPT

Giza

River Nile

UPPER EGYPT

Valley of the kings

Thebes

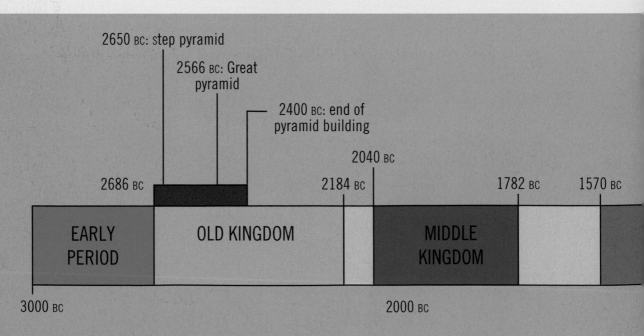

2650 BC: step pyramid

2566 BC: Great pyramid

2400 BC: end of pyramid building

2040 BC

2686 BC   2184 BC   1782 BC   1570 BC

EARLY PERIOD   OLD KINGDOM   MIDDLE KINGDOM

3000 BC   2000 BC

There were people living in Egypt over 5,000 years ago. People lived in small villages. Settlers came from the west, south, east, and northeast. They liked the valley of the River Nile, because they could catch fish and grow all sorts of crops there.

Ancient Egyptian **civilization** began around 3000 BC. This was when a king, called a **pharaoh**, began to rule the whole country. We divide Egyptian civilization into four periods. We call them the Early Period, the Old Kingdom, the Middle Kingdom, and the New Kingdom. You can see these periods marked on the timeline below. In between, there were wars. The pharaohs stopped ruling when the **Romans** took control in 30 BC.

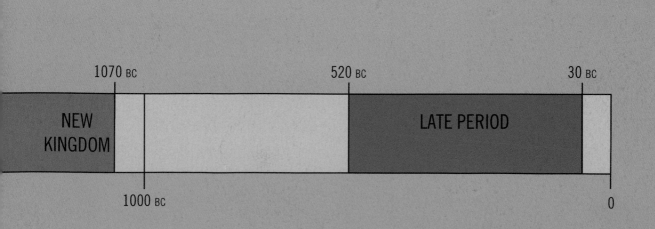

The River Nile

The Ancient Egyptians invented the shadoof, shown here, to lift water from the River Nile. Shadoofs are still used today.

The River Nile floods every year. As the water goes down, it leaves behind rich soil. The land that has been flooded is the only place where crops can grow.

The Egyptians wanted to grow more crops. But to do this they needed more water. They had to stop some of the flood water draining back into the river. This would allow them to make more fields. They also had to find a way to get water from the river all year round.

The Egyptians saw that the flood water could be held back with ponds and canals. Then they could use the water. It was hard work to dig the ponds and canals. The Egyptians had to clear and repair them all the time. They could only do this if they all worked together.

The Egyptians got more than water from the Nile. Here we see a nobleman hunting river birds to eat. The people also ate fish and used reeds to make baskets and boats.

Farming

The Egyptians farmed the land when the flood waters of the River Nile went down. They had to grow crops that would be cut before the next flood. The most important crops were wheat and barley, which were used to make bread and beer. These were what most Egyptians ate and drank.

Another important crop was **flax**, used to make cloth. The Egyptians also grew fruit and vegetables, too. They ate a lot of onions and garlic, dates, and grapes.

The ancient Egyptians grew grapes to eat and to make wine.

Farmers used animals to help them do the hard work in the fields.

The Egyptians kept geese and cows for their eggs and milk. They also hunted river birds and fish. They had no farm machines. Goats and sheep pressed the seed into the ground with their feet as soon as it was planted. An ox pulled the plough, and trampled the grain to get the **husks** off.

The pharaoh

The Egyptians had to work together to control the River Nile. This was the best way to grow plenty of food, so that everyone had enough to eat. People often work together better if there is someone in charge. This person can make sure that all the work is done at the right time. In Egypt this person was called the **pharaoh**. He was seen as more like a god than just a person.

Tutankhamen is the most famous of the pharaohs. He was only about eight years old when he became pharaoh. He is famous because his people hid his tomb so well that it is the only tomb of a pharaoh that has not been robbed. The tomb was found in 1922, full of treasures such as the **sarcophagus** shown here.

Pharaoh Tutankhamen's sarcophagus shows him holding signs for Upper and Lower Egypt. He has the goddesses of both parts on his crown. This is to show that he ruled all of Egypt.

Vulture, symbol
of goddess of
Upper Egypt

Cobra, symbol
of goddess of
Lower Egypt

Crook,
symbol
of Lower
Egypt

Flail,
symbol
of Upper
Egypt

How Egypt was ruled

The **scribes** were the only people who could write. This skill made them important, because they could check all the food that was stored. Here a scribe is counting the geese.

On the opposite page is a picture that shows how the Egyptians divided up the work. The **pharaoh** was at the top, giving out the work. Under him were the **viziers**, high priests, and nobles. The Egyptians thought that all jobs were important except for those of the slaves, who were at the bottom. Slaves were mostly prisoners captured in battles.

Pharaoh

Queen

Nobles

Grand Viziers of Upper
and Lower Egypt

High Priest and
High Priestess

Governor

Craftsmen   Artists

Scribes   Tax Gatherers

Priests   Priestesses

Builders   Farmers

Scribes

Wab

Slaves

Trade

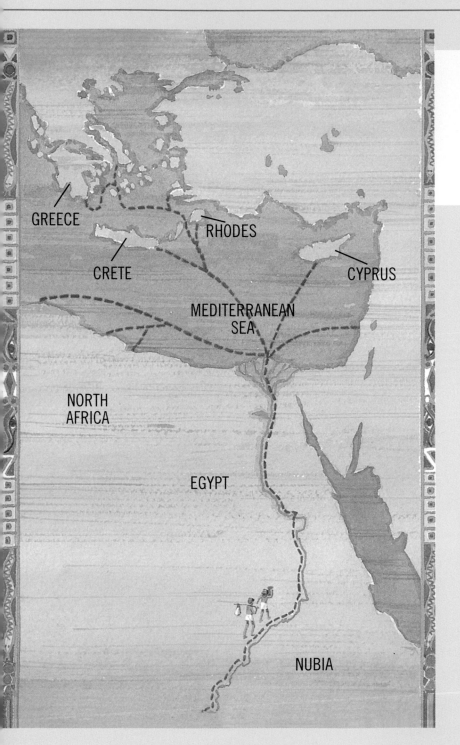

GREECE

RHODES

CRETE

CYPRUS

MEDITERRANEAN
SEA

NORTH
AFRICA

EGYPT

NUBIA

This map shows places with which the Egyptians traded.

The Egyptians did different jobs. Some were farmers, and others were fishermen. Some made shoes, while some brewed beer and made bread. They did not have money to buy these things from each other. Instead, they **traded** with each other to get the things that they wanted.

Markets were often located by the river. They were where most trading was done.

The Egyptians also traded with other countries. They made more rope and fibre from **flax** than they needed. They often had more wheat than they would need in the coming year. They traded their extra supplies for things that they did not have, such as wood, olive oil, silver and gold. They traded with other countries in the Mediterranean, travelling mostly by boat.

Gods and goddesses

The Egyptians had lots of gods. Some of the gods were known all over Egypt. Other gods were only known by people in a certain area. The Egyptians saw important things, such as the Sun or the River Nile, as gods. In pictures, they often showed their gods with animal heads.

Egyptians prayed to different gods at different times. If they thought that the River Nile was not going to flood, they prayed to the river goddess, Hapi. If a child was ill, they prayed to Bes, god of children, or Imhotep, god of medicine.

Hunefer Anubis Anubis Ammut Thoth

Every Egyptian house had its own **shrine**. This was a place where people could pray at any time.

The Egyptians also built huge **temples**. These were painted with pictures of stories about the gods. Each temple had a room where a statue of the god was kept. Only the priests were allowed to see it. Ordinary people were not allowed into the big temples. They left gifts outside for the gods.

The gods judge a dead man (Hunefer). They balance his heart against the feather of truth. If he has been good, he can go to the Fields of Iaru (Heaven). If he has been bad, Ammut eats him.

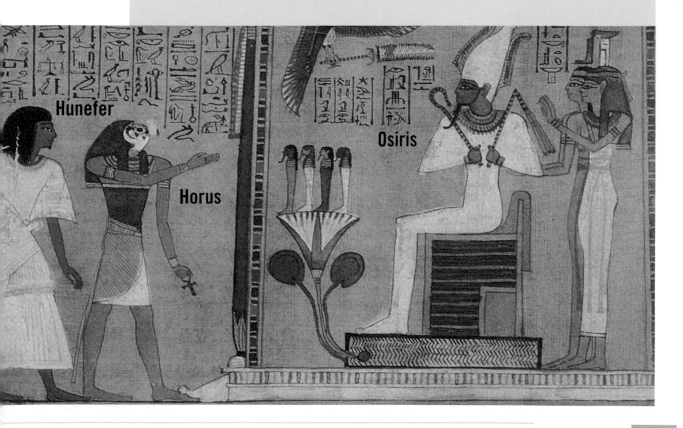

Mummies

These Egyptian priests are oiling and wrapping a body.

The Egyptians thought that people who died went to a new world. They would need their bodies in the new world, so their bodies had to be kept from going bad. To do this, the Egyptians first removed the soft insides. They covered the body with a type of salt, to dry it out. They rubbed oils on it. Then they wrapped layers of cloth around it. A body that has been treated in this way is called a **mummy**.

They sometimes gave the mummy a face mask. It looked like the person did in real life. A rich person would have their jewels put on it. The mummy was put in a painted case called a **sarcophagus**. It was then buried in the ground or put in a tomb. Only some of the first **pharaohs** had **pyramids**. Most of them were buried in tombs cut in the rock in the Valley of the Kings.

A priestess in her sarcophagus, which shows what she looked like.

Pyramids

Pyramids were built out of big stone blocks. The blocks had to be dug up and cut to size. Then they had to be moved to the right place by sliding them along on wooden rollers. It took lots of men many years to build a pyramid.

The stone blocks had to be dragged up ramps that got higher and higher.

The Great Pyramid.
It took 5,000 men
20 years to build.
It is made from
over 2.3 million
blocks of stone.

The **mummy** of the dead **pharaoh** was put into a small room in the middle of the pyramid. He had lots of things he might need for his next life. There were jewels, food, furniture, pots, and even model dolls to work for him. The entrances were closed up, but the pyramids were often robbed, so the workers made secret rooms to bury the pharaohs in, with traps to catch the thieves.

Everyday life

Egyptian life had a pattern. All the women worked in the home. Most Egyptian men worked at two jobs. When the water in the Nile was low, they worked on the land. When the Nile flooded, the men had other jobs. Some were builders or fishermen. Others were artists or jewellers. Only the most important people and the priests did not farm.

Egyptians had very little furniture.

Egyptian clothes looked a lot like this. The big lumps on the women's heads are scented lumps of fat. They melted in the heat and ran down the women's faces. This kept them cool and made them smell nice.

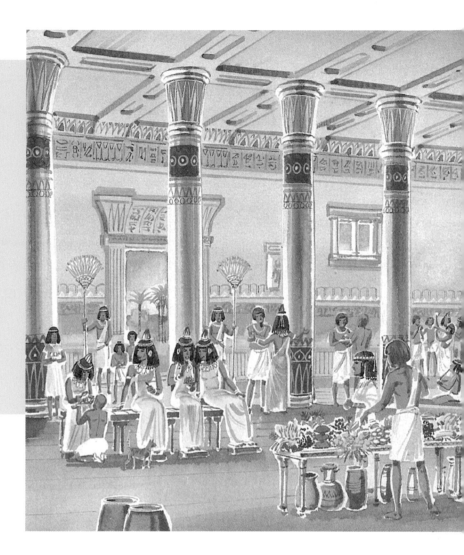

It was very hot in Egypt, so people did not wear many clothes. Men, women, and children wore either thin cloth **kilts** or robes. Women wore as much makeup and jewellery as they could afford.

To stay cool, people shaved off all their hair. They wore wigs on special occasions.

Houses

The Egyptians built all houses in the same way. They used mud bricks for building. The walls were thick, to keep out the heat. The houses of important people had more rooms. They had lovely painted walls inside, but they looked the same on the outside.

Because it did not rain very often, there was no need to have sloping roofs to carry the rain away. The flat roofs were part of the house. People sat on their roofs, or dried washing there. Most people cooked outside, so if they had no garden they did their cooking on the roof.

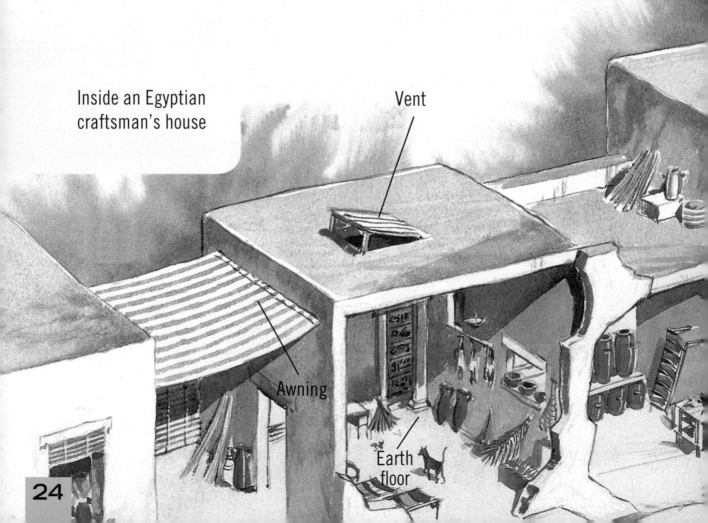

Inside an Egyptian craftsman's house

Vent

Awning

Earth floor

The houses had rooms under the ground. These rooms were dark and cool. They were very good for storing food and drink.

Model of an Egyptian house

Shrine

Mud bread oven

Cellar

Children

Children in Egypt grew up to do the same jobs as their parents. Girls stayed at home with their mothers. They learned how to look after the house, bake bread, and weave **flax**. Boys went to work with their fathers and helped as much as they could. They only went to school if they were going to work as a **scribe**.

Egyptian children worked hard.

Here are some Egyptian children's toys. They are made from wood and reeds.

Very young children stayed at home with their mothers. Many of their games were like games today. They played racing games, tag, and leapfrog. They had balls and wooden toys. Older children played a game like chess, called senet.

Medicine

An Egyptian doctor had many tools.

Making **mummies** helped the Egyptians learn how the body worked. They saw the lungs, heart, and other organs when they took them out of the body. This helped them to think of better cures for sick people.

The Egyptians tried to make people better in different ways. They made medicines from plants. They treated snake bites by sucking the poison from the wound. They tried to keep clean. Everyone tried to wash their clothes and dishes often.

Egyptians carried magic charms with them to keep illness and evil away.

The Egyptians also believed in magic. They thought that evil **spirits** made people ill. They prayed to a god to make the spirits go away. They drank magic drinks to make them well. They wore magic charms to keep evil spirits away.

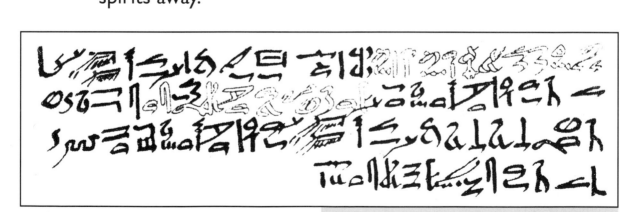

The magic potion recipe above calls for beetles and a snake's head.

29

End of the empire

Egypt became part of the Greek **empire** in 332 BC. This changed the way people in Egypt lived. Three hundred years later the **Romans** took control of Egypt. Slowly, the Egyptians gave up their special way of life and the **pharaohs** stopped ruling. This was the end of the ancient Egyptian **civilization**.

This is an Egyptian mummy case but the painting of the face is a Roman painting. The two cultures mixed when the Romans took control of Egypt.

Glossary

civilization the way of life of a group of people

empire group of territories or lands controlled by one country

flax plant that can be made into cloth

husk the hard outer covering of a grain such as wheat

kilt type of skirt worn by men or women

mummy dead body that has been specially treated and wrapped in cloth so that it doesn't rot away

pharaoh the ruler of an ancient Egyptian kingdom

pyramid structure that has a square base and sloping triangular sides that meet at the top

Romans the people of the ancient Roman Empire (500 BC – AD 476)

sarcophagus painted case in which a mummy was stored

scribe person whose job it was to read, write, and keep records

shrine special place for worshipping a god or gods

spirits magical beings or forces that we cannot see

temple building for religious worship

trade to swap one type of item for another instead of buying and selling using money

viziers men who worked for the pharaoh and had a lot of power

Find out more

Books to read
Hands on Ancient History: Ancient Egypt, Alexandra Fix (Heinemann Library, 2006)
Picture the Past: Life along the River Nile, Jane Shuter (Heinemann Library, 2005)

Using the Internet
Explore the Internet to find out more about the ancient Egyptians. Use a search engine, such as www.yahooligans.com or www.internet4kids.com and type in a keyword or phrase such as "Tutankhamen" or "pyramids".

Index